Tell Your Parents

How to Harness

SOLAR

POWER

for Your Home

WITHDRAWN

Solar-powered
Floralis Genérica
in Buenos Aires,
Argentina

STEPHANIE BEARCE

Mitchell Lane
PUBLISHERS

P.O. Box 196
Hockessin, Delaware 19707
Visit us on the web: www.mitchelllane.com
Comments? email us: mitchelllane@mitchelllane.com

Fitchburg Public Library
5530 Lacy Road
Fitchburg, WI 53711

Mitchell Lane

PUBLISHERS

Tell Your Parents

How to Harness Solar Power for Your Home
How to Use Wind Power to Light and Heat Your Home
All About Electric and Hybrid Cars
Green Changes You Can Make Around Your Home
How You Can Use Waste Energy to Heat
and Light Your Home

Copyright © 2010 by Mitchell Lane Publishers

All rights reserved. No part of this book may be reproduced without written permission from the publisher. Printed and bound in the United States of America.

Printing   2   3   4   5   6   7   8   9

Library of Congress
Cataloging-in-Publication Data
Bearce, Stephanie.
  How to harness solar power for your home / by Stephanie Bearce.
      p. cm. — (Tell your parents)
  Includes bibliographical references and index.
  ISBN 978-1-58415-761-8 (library bound)
  1. Solar energy—Juvenile literature. I. Title.
  TJ810.3.B43 2009
  621.47—dc22
                                    2009004529

PUBLISHER'S NOTE: The facts on which the story in this book is based have been thoroughly researched. Documentation of such research can be found on page 44. While every possible effort has been made to ensure accuracy, the publisher will not assume liability for damages caused by inaccuracies in the data, and makes no warranty on the accuracy of the information contained herein.

To reflect current usage, we have chosen to use the secular era designations BCE ("before the common era") and CE ("of the common era") instead of the traditional designations BC ("before Christ") and AD (*anno Domini*, "in the year of the Lord").

About the running heads: The toys in the running heads are all solar powered.

PLB/ PLB2

CONTENTS

Ed Begley Jr. peers into his solar oven

GOING SOLAR

On a sunny day in California, you can find actor Ed Begley Jr. cooking soup in his backyard. He's not cooking over a fire, and he's not using electricity. Ed Begley cooks with a **solar energy** oven. It is a shiny metal box that uses solar reflectors to catch the light of the sun to heat food. If Ed is cooking a big meal, he must move the oven every couple of hours as the sun moves across the sky. The oven works quite efficiently. It heats up to 375 degrees Fahrenheit. That's hot enough to cook a pizza.

Ed Begley believes solar energy is a sensible way to make electricity. Energy from the sun is free. It is clean, and it doesn't cause pollution. Best of all, solar energy is **renewable**. As long as the sun keeps shining, there will always be a supply of solar energy.

Edward Norton inspects solar panels

Traditional home with solar panels

As a kid in the 1970s, Ed Begley lived in the San Fernando Valley of California. During that time the area was very polluted. The air was so dirty, it looked like gray fog even on sunny days. Ed decided that when he grew up, he would try to help make the planet cleaner.

As a young man, he stopped driving a car. He rode his bicycle everywhere, or he took the bus. He even rode his bicycle to the television and movie studios where he worked. Ed believed he could help keep the air clean by not using gasoline-powered vehicles, which pollute the air. He also taught other people about air pollution.

As Ed studied and learned more about helping the environment, he learned about solar power—the energy in the heat and light of the sun. Energy in the sun's heat is called **solar thermal energy**. It can be collected and used to warm

a house or to heat water. If you have ever picked up a garden hose that was lying in the sun and felt warm water run out of it, you have felt solar thermal energy at work.

When the light of the sun is used to make electricity, it is called **photovoltaic (PV) energy**. This type of electricity can be used to run household appliances. In 1990, Ed installed solar panels on the roof of his California home. The solar panels collect the light from the sun and use it to make electricity. Ed then uses the electricity to power his

Ed Begley Jr. stands in his backyard vegetable garden at his home, which sports a solar oven, water recycling system, and solar panels on the roof.

lights and run his refrigerator and other appliances. He even uses solar energy to charge his pollution-free electric car.

On bright sunny days, the solar panels on Ed's house make more electricity than he can use. The extra electricity is stored in batteries in Ed's garage. The batteries can supply electricity to Ed's house on days when it is cloudy. He also plugs his electric car into the batteries. This charges his car so that Ed never has to use gasoline.

Ed Begley Jr. is just one of many famous people around the world who are working to make planet Earth a healthier place to live by using solar energy. Johnny Depp, Scarlett

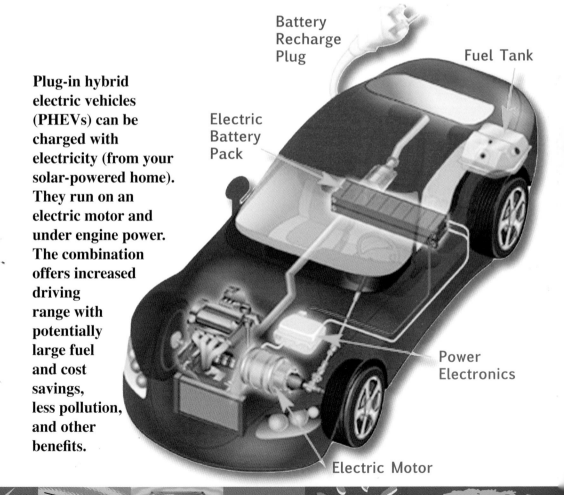

Plug-in hybrid electric vehicles (PHEVs) can be charged with electricity (from your solar-powered home). They run on an electric motor and under engine power. The combination offers increased driving range with potentially large fuel and cost savings, less pollution, and other benefits.

Battery Recharge Plug

Fuel Tank

Electric Battery Pack

Power Electronics

Electric Motor

U.S. Energy Consumption by Source, 2007

BIOMASS   3.6%

renewable

Heating, electricity, transportation

PETROLEUM   37.5%

nonrenewable

Transporation, manufacturing

HYDROPOWER   2.4%

renewable

Electricity

NATURAL GAS   23.3%

nonrenewable

Heating, manufacturing, electricity

GEOTHERMAL   0.3%

renewable

Heating, electricity

COAL   22.5%

nonrenewable

Electricity, manufacturing

WIND   0.3%

renewable

Electricity

URANIUM   8.3%

nonrenewable

Electricity

SOLAR   0.1%

renewable

Light, heating, electricity

PROPANE   1.7%

nonrenewable

Manufacturing, heating

Source: Energy Information Administration, Annual Energy Review, 2007

Over 90 percent of the energy used in the United States comes from nonrenewable sources. Even small increases in the use of renewable energy can help reduce carbon air pollution and save valuable resources.

Johansson, and Orlando Bloom are three people who agree with Ed Begley Jr. Each of these actors has installed solar panels in his or her home. They use solar power to run their televisions, microwaves, and dishwashers. They believe that by using solar energy in their homes, they can reduce the amount of pollution on the earth.

Most electricity is made by burning **fossil fuels** such as coal and petroleum. When fossil fuels are burned, they release

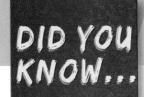

DID YOU KNOW...

Enough sunlight falls on the earth every minute to meet the world's energy demands for an entire year. Using the power of the sun to make energy is not a new idea. Scientist Albert Einstein received the Nobel Prize in Physics in 1921 in part for figuring out the law of the photoelectric effect. The law of the photoelectric effect describes how sunlight can cause electricity to flow.

pollutants into the air. Fossil fuels are also **nonrenewable**, meaning there is a limited amount of them in the earth. When it is used up, there will be no more. Many people believe that using renewable solar energy is a good alternative to using fossil fuels.

So why haven't more people switched to solar power? One problem with solar energy is the cost. Solar panels are very expensive to buy and install. In 2009, installing a set of solar panels—enough to power an 1,800-square-foot-home—cost about $30,000. Actor Edward Norton realized this was too much money for most people. He wanted to help people who could not afford to buy their own solar power systems, so he formed an organization to help low-income families get solar energy for their homes. His group, called BP Solar Neighbors, works with other actors to buy solar panels for low-income family homes in Los Angeles, California. Whenever a celebrity signs up to buy a BP solar power system, the company also puts a system on the house of a low-income family.

The families who receive the solar power systems can save nearly $1,000 a year on their energy bills. Thanks to Ed Norton and BP Solar Neighbors, low-income families can get low-cost solar energy. The solar power system saves the family money, and it also lets them help make planet Earth a healthier place to live.

Ed Norton hopes that other families will see the benefits of solar power and install the systems on their homes. The electricity savings can be higher on larger homes and buildings. You can use the chart below to help you calculate how much energy you could save in your home or school if the building used solar power.

AMPAD
evidence.
RECYCLED.

Annual Electricity Bill Savings
Kilowatts of electricity generated from PV per year
X   Kilowatt hours used per year
=   Annual Kilowatt energy from the PV system

Annual Kilowatt energy from the PV system
X   Current residential electricity rate
=   Annual dollars saved

According to the Energy Information Administration, by the end of 2008, the average cost of electricity in U.S. homes was about 11 cents per kilowatt hour.

Prince Charles of England is also interested in building houses that use solar energy. He believes that solar energy, along with other green energy sources, will help the planet. "Green" energy is renewable energy. It is energy that will not run out and does not pollute or harm the planet in other ways. Wind is another renewable energy source. Using solar and wind energy together works well in places that do not get a lot of sun.

In England, Prince Charles is working with construction companies to build whole neighborhoods that use solar power. These homes will have the modern conveniences of lights, heat, and appliances, but they will reduce their **carbon footprint** on the earth.

A carbon footprint is the amount of carbons put into the air by different activities. People leave personal carbon footprints. Every time a person uses electricity, he or she puts carbons into the air. If that person drives a gasoline-powered car, the car releases carbons and adds to his or her footprint. Carbons cause pollution, so it is important for each person to reduce the amount of them he or she puts into the atmosphere. Solar energy gives off fewer carbons than other forms of energy. Using solar energy reduces a person's carbon footprint.

Prince Charles doesn't just ask other people to use solar power. He has solar panels on his home in England. He is also building a house for his son, Prince William, that uses green technology, including solar panels.

Prince Charles, Ed Norton, and Ed Begley Jr. all believe that as more people and governments realize the value of using solar energy, the demand for the panels will increase. As more people want them, the manufacturers will find ways to build them at lower cost. Then more people will be able to afford solar energy for their homes.

Baking in a solar oven

WHY TRY SOLAR?

What is the first thing you do when you get home from school? Turn on the computer? Open the refrigerator? Click on the television set? Refrigerators, computers, and televisions are a part of everyday life in the United States. We are used to being able to turn on a fan or flick on the lights whenever we need them. But without electricity, most of our modern conveniences would not work. Without electricity, we would still be using candles and fireplaces to light and heat our homes.

The electricity we use in our homes is a **secondary energy source**. This means it takes another type of energy to make electricity. Power plants use a **primary energy source** for fuel, such as coal, oil, natural gas, wind, water, and the sun. These are natural energy sources. These primary

Generators in a hydroelectric power plant

Polar bears and other animals' habitats are threatened by global warming

energy sources are used to run generators, which make electricity for homes and businesses.

A generator creates electricity through **electromagnetic induction**. This principal was discovered by Michael Faraday in 1831. Faraday discovered that if an electricity conductor, like a wire, is moved through a magnetic field, an electric current will flow. As a coil of wire spins around a magnet (or a magnet spins within the coil), an electric current is induced to flow through the wire. This electric current is then sent through wires from the electric power plant to houses and buildings.

Electric power stations often use **turbines** to drive a generator. A turbine looks like a large fan. Coal, oil, and natural gas are burned in large furnaces to heat water. The

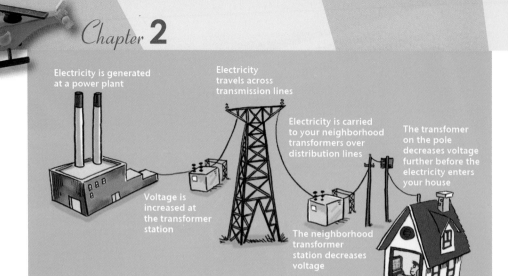

Electricity is generated at a power plant

Electricity travels across transmission lines

Electricity is carried to your neighborhood transformers over distribution lines

The transfomer on the pole decreases voltage further before the electricity enters your house

Voltage is increased at the transformer station

The neighborhood transformer station decreases voltage

Electricity has to travel a long way to get from the power plant to your home. Sometimes it must travel hundreds of miles before it can light up your home.

steam from the hot water pushes on the blades of the turbine. As the turbine spins, it moves gears and shafts that are connected to a generator, which makes the generator spin also. The generator converts the mechanical (moving) energy of the spinning turbine into electric energy.

In 2007, sixty-six percent of all the electricity in the United States was made by burning coal or natural gas. This worked for many years, but finding more coal and petroleum on earth is difficult. Most of the oil fields in the United States were discovered by 1930. Worldwide, oil field discoveries peaked in 1973. Geologists now find new oil reserves at a rate of only one barrel of oil for every four that we consume.

Supplies of coal, oil, and natural gas are nonrenewable—they are limited, and they are dwindling quickly. Scientists believe that oil may run out by the year 2050; natural gas by 2075; and coal by 2300. Even though 300 years sounds like a long time, it is important to think about people living in the future. If your great-great-grandchildren will be relying on electricity for their lifestyle, alternative fuels must be found before traditional fuels run out.

Meanwhile, the planet suffers from the emission of carbons into the air. In 2007, the world put over 27 million tons of carbon dioxide into the air. If we continue to put that much pollution in the air every year for 300 years, those same great-great-grandchildren will have a very dirty earth.

Coal- and oil-fueled electric power plants are the largest source of air pollution in the United States. They produce about 2.2 billion tons of carbon dioxide pollution each year.

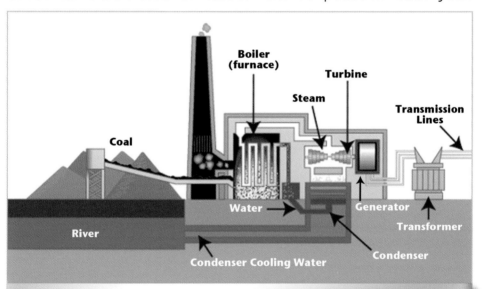

In a coal-fueled power plant, coal is burned to boil water. The steam produced by the boiling water moves the turbine, which generates electricity. Burning coal releases carbon into the air.

DID YOU KNOW...

Nuclear power plants emit less than one one-hundredth of the carbon dioxide that is produced by coal or gas-powered stations. Nuclear power plants pay back the energy required to build them in less than two months of operation. And there is enough radioactive fuel—uranium and thorium—to run nuclear plants for hundreds of centuries. However, as nuclear power plants operate, radioactive waste is produced. Radioactive waste has been proven to cause cancer in humans and animals. It is hard to dispose of and can be harmful to the earth for thousands of years.

They also release 12 million tons of sulfur dioxide and 7 million tons of nitrogen oxides. All of these chemicals mix with the air. This air pollution is believed to cause asthma, lung diseases, and even cancer.

Another problem with traditional electric power plants is that they are not efficient. When coal is burned to make electricity, it is only one-third efficient. This means that two-thirds of the electricity made by a coal electricity plant is lost before it reaches any users. Power plants have to make three times as much energy as people use, adding more pollution to the air and water than they would if the systems were more efficient.

Too much carbon dioxide in the air may also cause the temperature on the earth to rise. The earth is covered with a blanket of air called the atmosphere. In the atmosphere are many different gases. One of those gases is oxygen—the gas that humans and animals breathe. Another gas, carbon dioxide, absorbs the heat from the sun. It traps the heat and keeps it on the earth, just as heat is trapped inside a car on a warm day. This is called the **greenhouse effect**. The greenhouse effect is what makes the earth warm enough to grow plants and keep animals alive. Without some carbon dioxide, there would be no life on earth.

But you can have too much of a good thing. The more carbon dioxide there is in the atmosphere, the more heat is trapped on the earth. Too much carbon dioxide can make the planet too hot. This is called **global warming**. Plants and animals cannot survive when temperatures get too high.

Scientists have been keeping track of the temperature of the earth. They have found that earth's average temperature is increasing. A change of only a few degrees can have a big effect on the planet.

For example, as the temperature increases, the polar ice caps begin to melt. The meltwater raises the levels of the oceans. As the ocean levels rise, towns and cities near the coast can flood. Many people could get hurt or lose their homes. Many animals could be killed by floods and the loss of living space.

Causes of Global Warming

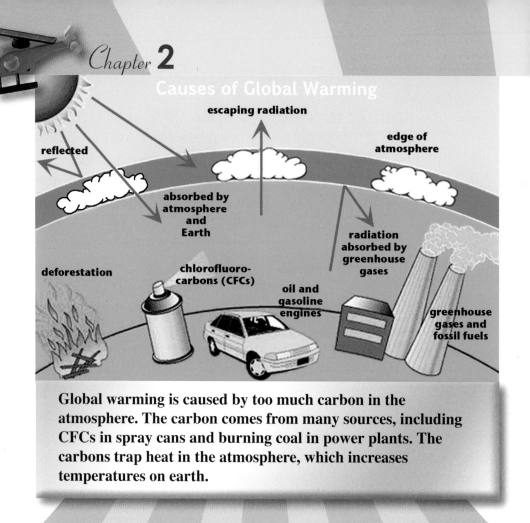

escaping radiation

edge of atmosphere

reflected

absorbed by atmosphere and Earth

radiation absorbed by greenhouse gases

deforestation

chlorofluoro-carbons (CFCs)

oil and gasoline engines

greenhouse gases and fossil fuels

Global warming is caused by too much carbon in the atmosphere. The carbon comes from many sources, including CFCs in spray cans and burning coal in power plants. The carbons trap heat in the atmosphere, which increases temperatures on earth.

Increasing temperatures can also threaten plants. Plants need to have the correct temperatures to grow. If the temperatures change, whole species of plants will die. Without the plants and trees for food and shelter, many animals will become **extinct**, too. Global warming is a serious problem, and using coal and oil adds to it.

People looking to decrease land and water pollution, and the effects of global warming, have found that solar power is a possible solution. While solar panels may be somewhat expensive for individual homeowners, it is possible for businesses and corporations to begin using solar energy right now. Installing solar power systems on large buildings can be one way to make immediate use of solar energy. In Australia, the Crowne Plaza Hotel at Alice Springs has installed one of the world's largest building-mounted solar arrays. The hotel has monitors that tell guests how much energy is being produced and used. The owners of the hotel hope that more businesses will follow their example and go solar.

Scientists continue to look for ways to make solar power less expensive and more available to individuals. For example, solar windows are being produced by companies in both California and Australia. The windows are made by placing a special light-absorbing dye between two plates of glass. When light strikes the dye, it excites the electrons in the dye, and their movement creates an electric current. The windows can be installed in homes and offices. Solar glass is also used to power some cars, such as the Italdesign Quaranta, a concept car revealed in 2008.

Solar windows are not as efficient as solar panels, but they are about one-third the cost, and they can be used over the entire surface of a building. A skyscraper covered in solar windows could generate a vast amount of electricity.

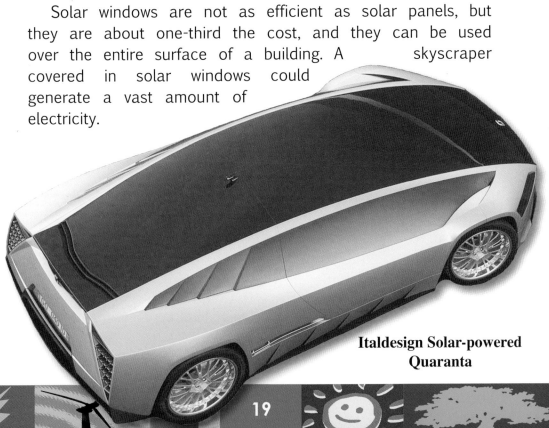

Italdesign Solar-powered Quaranta

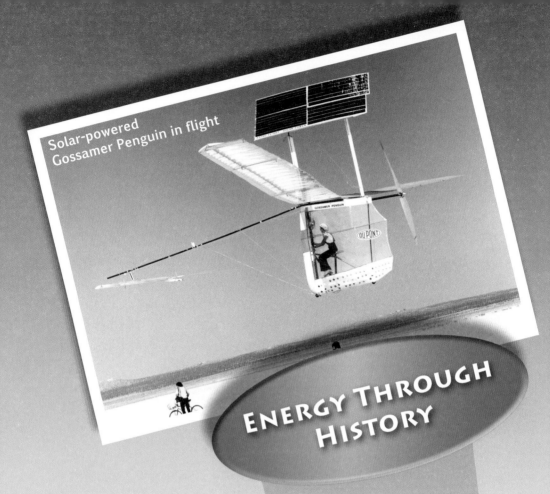

Solar-powered Gossamer Penguin in flight

Energy Through History

For most of history, people used wood to heat their homes and cook their food. Prehistoric people built fires from wood to give their caves heat and light. Over two thousand years ago, people in China used petroleum to light lamps for their houses. In the 1400s, people started burning coal in their fireplaces.

In 1752, Benjamin Franklin started experimenting with electricity. Franklin had long suspected that lightning was an electrical current, and he wanted to see if he was right. He thought he could test his idea by seeing if lightning would pass through metal the way electricity does. He decided to use a metal key. He needed a way to get the key close to some lightning, so he tied it to the string of a kite. Then he waited for lightning. He got his chance in a June thunderstorm. When lightning struck near the kite, the air was full of

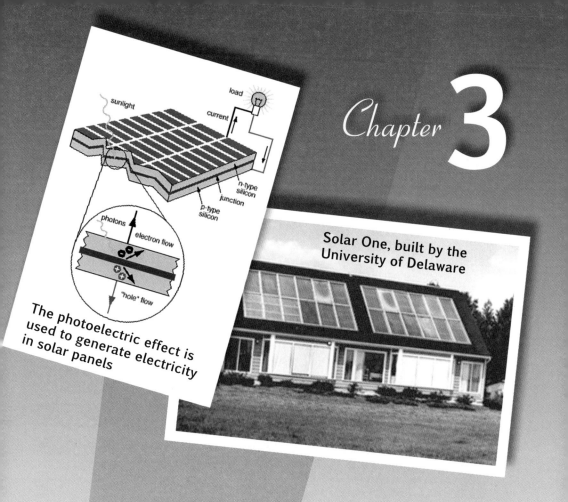

The photoelectric effect is used to generate electricity in solar panels

Solar One, built by the University of Delaware

electricity, and it traveled through the key. Franklin had his proof.

His discovery helped scientists understand how electricity could be used for energy. Other inventors were able to use this knowledge to make machines that used electricity. For example, Thomas Edison invented the electric lightbulb in 1879, and people stopped using kerosene lamps and gaslights. The new electric lights were safer. They didn't cause fires. They were also much brighter and cleaner. Soon nearly everyone wanted electricity in their homes.

Electric power plants were built to supply electricity for lights. As electricity became more available, scientists found more ways to use it. The electric refrigerator was made available for home use in 1915. The refrigerator kept food cold and stopped it from spoiling. Radios using electricity

Chapter 3

In 1800, Italian scientist Alessandro Volta discovered the first practical method of generating electricity. His voltaic pile consisted of alternating discs of zinc and copper, with pieces of cardboard in between each pair of discs. The cardboard was soaked in salty water. Volta attached a wire to each end of the voltaic pile. When the wires were connected to each other, an electric current flowed. This was the first electric battery. Battery power is still measured in volts.

became popular in the 1920s. For the first time, people living miles away from Washington, D.C., could hear the president give his speeches. They could get news from across the country as it was happening instead of waiting for newspapers to be printed. Electricity changed the world—and people wanted more electricity to run all their new inventions.

Now, at the beginning of the twenty-first century, people all over the world are using electricity for their television sets, computers, and microwave ovens. They use electricity for their washing machines and vacuum cleaners. They even want electricity to make their morning toast. As more people demand electricity, producing it in the traditional way is getting more expensive. The resources used to run electric power plants, such as oil and coal, are harder to find. This makes them more valuable and much more expensive. Solar power is becoming more attractive to energy companies. There is an abundant supply of sunshine, and it does not have to be mined or drilled.

Serious development of solar cells in the United States began in 1954 in Bell Labs. Scientists Daryl Chapin, Calvin Fuller, and Gerald Pearson were working on the silicon voltaic cell. It was the first solar cell capable of changing enough

Explorer VI was one of the first satellites to use solar panels for its energy source. Launched in 1959, it had four solar cell paddles. It orbited Earth until July 1961.

sunlight into electricity to be able to run everyday electrical appliances.

In 1959, silicon solar cells were used on the *Explorer VI* satellite. The solar panels produced the electricity necessary to keep the satellite running as it orbited Earth. Solar cells have been used on most satellites since that time.

In the 1970s, Elliot Berman designed a solar cell that greatly reduced the cost of solar energy. His new solar cells were still expensive, but they could be used in places where it was very difficult to run electric lines. Dr. Berman's solar cells were used to power lights and horns in lighthouses and at railroad crossings. They were also used to power lights on offshore oil rigs.

In 1973, the University of Delaware built Solar One. It was the first house that used solar panels to make electricity. The house had solar panels on the roof. The panels made electricity for the home during the day, but at night the house used electricity from a traditional electric plant.

During the 1980s and '90s, scientists worked on ways to improve the efficiency of solar cells. Their goal was to get the cost of solar energy low enough for the average person to afford. They made many exciting discoveries. In 1981, the first solar-powered airplane flew over the English Channel. In 1996, the house Solar Two was built. This time the house had solar storage batteries. It could use solar electricity even when there was no sun.

Scientists improved solar cells, and people began building solar power plants in desert areas. Acres of solar panels were placed in sunny locations. They began collecting the sun's energy and storing it as electricity. This electricity could then be used by homes and businesses to power lights and appliances.

Since then, amazing things have been done with solar technology. The National Aeronautics and Space Administration (NASA) has developed a special type of airplane called the Helios. The Helios has wings covered in solar cells. In 2001, this plane set the record for non–rocket powered aircraft. It traveled more than 18 miles high into the atmosphere.

The International Space Station has a huge **solar array** that produces electricity for the station. Homes now have solar panels on their roofs to make electricity. Cars have been developed that can use batteries that are charged by solar energy, solar panels, or solar glass.

Scientists believe that one of the best energy sources for the future will be solar power. The desert southwest of the United States is an incredible resource for sunlight. Scientists and inventors believe that solar collectors built there could produce at least half of the electricity used by the United States.

As solar cells are used more and more by big industry, their cost gets lower. This is because of mass production. If only a few people want solar panels, the companies that produce them have to charge them for the operating costs. If thousands of people want solar panels, the operating cost of building the panels is divided among more people. This reduces the overall cost for each user.

Helios

The lights on this street are powered by solar panels and wind turbines

HOW DOES SOLAR POWER WORK?

You have probably used some things that are powered by solar cells. Many calculators have solar cells on them. The calculator works when it is in the light. The solar cells change the light into electricity. That electricity helps you solve math problems.

You can also see solar cells at work around you. Many states have installed small solar panels on street and highway lights. During the day, the panels collect and store electricity. Then when it is dark, the stored electricity powers the lights. People use smaller versions of these to light the walkways to their homes.

All of this solar power sounds good. It stops pollution. It is a renewable resource. It saves oil and energy. But how does it work?

A solar calculator. Want a bite?

Solar water heater

With photovoltaic or active solar energy, sunlight captured by solar panels is converted into electricity. Solar electric panels are made of **silicon**, which is found in sand. There is more silicon on the earth than almost anything else. It is easy to find, so it seems like it would make solar energy very cheap. But making a solar panel is very hard to do, and it is expensive.

The first step in making a solar panel is to create silicon wafers. Quartz, which is a mineral made from silicon and carbon dioxide, is placed in a special oven called an electric arc furnace. This furnace heats the quartz to 1,000 degrees Fahrenheit. The silicon melts and the carbon dioxide turns to gas. This process makes silicon that is 99 percent pure—but that is not pure enough for solar panels.

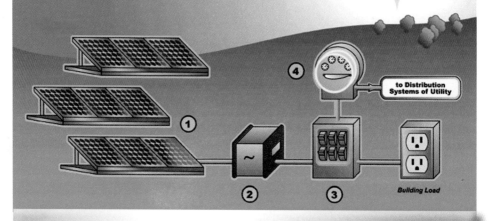

Chapter 4

1. Photovoltaic Array converts solar energy to direct current electricity
2. Inverter converts direct current to alternating current
3. Breaker box provides an interconnection point to the consumer or grid
4. Meter measures the energy from the solar array and the building load

to Distribution Systems of Utility

Building Load

When sunlight hits the photovoltaic (solar) array, it excites the electrons and creates electricity. The electricity moves through the inverter, where it is turned into alternating current. Breaker boxes connect electricity to the grid or homes, and meters measure the electricity being used.

The silicon must go through another firing in the furnace. This time it is pulled or dragged through the furnace so that the remaining impurities go to one end of the silicon piece. That end is removed.

The pure silicon is formed into a cylinder, which is sliced into very thin wafers. The wafers look like skinny CDs. These silicon wafers are then stacked to make a solar panel called a photovoltaic panel or cell. When sunlight shines on the silicon wafers, it makes electrons in the wafers move. These moving electrons go through wires built into the solar panel, then they flow as electricity.

The panels are attached to the electrical system of the house. When a solar-home owner turns on the lights, the power comes from the solar panels on the roof of his house, and not from the electric company.

Large-scale use of solar power takes a great deal of land, because the solar panels must be laid out in a solar array.

U.S. President Barack Obama visits Nellis Air Force Base in Nevada. The base has built a solar array that has over 72,000 solar panels. This solar plant provides about 25 percent of the electricity needed for the 12,000 people who live and work on the base. It will save the air force nearly $1 million per year.

An array is a large number of solar panels connected together to gather and store energy from the sun. These solar panels are placed where they will receive a large amount of daily sunlight, such as the deserts of southern California and Nevada. (In one town in Spain, they placed their solar panels over a cemetery.) The electricity that is made from the solar array is then sold to homeowners to power their houses. This is an efficient way to provide electricity that does not pollute or use up oil and coal.

Some electric companies are experimenting with using the sun through a combination of solar panels and mirrors. This is called CSP, or concentrating solar power. Unlike photovoltaic power, which uses silicon wafers to convert sunlight directly into electricity, CSP plants generate electricity using heat. The mirrors are used to focus the sun's energy, sort of like a magnifying glass. The heat from the sun is concentrated onto a large container of oil. The superheated oil is used to generate steam, which drives a turbine to make electricity.

When it is dark, power can still be generated at CSP plants. Excess heat is stored in large insulated tanks filled with liquid (molten) salt. Two big advantages of these thermal power plants are that the electricity generation does not produce any carbons, and the sun's heat is free. These power plants, like solar arrays, need to be built in warm sunny areas such as the deserts of America's Southwest or Africa's Sahara. The United States, Spain, India, Egypt, Morocco, Mexico, Algeria, and Australia are developing CSP plants.

The PS10 concentrated solar power plant in Seville, Spain, has a 40-story-high concrete tower that collects the sunlight reflected by 624 giant mirrors. When construction of five additional CSP plants is completed in 2013, they will provide enough electricity for 180,000 homes.

As wonderful as solar power seems to be, there are a few disadvantages. Even with current technological advances, the cost to produce solar panels is high. Proponents of solar energy point out that the upfront expense of building and installing solar panels will eventually be made up by the cost savings in energy. But many companies and individuals just do not have the money for those upfront costs.

Also, carbon dioxide is emitted when silicon wafers are produced. People who are for solar power argue that the small amount of carbon dioxide put into the air by making

Bolivia

India

Kenya

Nepal

Mali

West Africa

People in many countries use solar power for cooking. Solar ovens can be made from simple materials such as cardboard and aluminum foil.

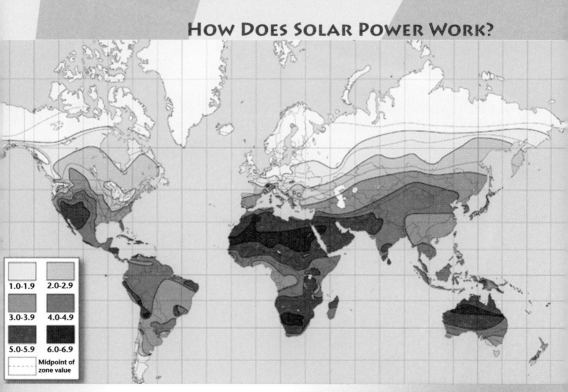

1.0-1.9	2.0-2.9
3.0-3.9	4.0-4.9
5.0-5.9	6.0-6.9
	Midpoint of zone value

The amount of sunlight (in hours per day) varies around the world. Even during the least sunny times of the year, some parts of the world receive more than enough sunshine to make solar power a good energy option.

solar panels is justifiable because the solar panels save much more carbon than they produce.

Finally, solar power is not always available. In some areas of the world, there are many cloudy days and low levels of sunlight. And the sun doesn't shine at night. This limits the time and places where solar power can be used. But solar power advocates believe that where solar energy is available, it should be used. Overall it is a cleaner and less wasteful form of energy production.

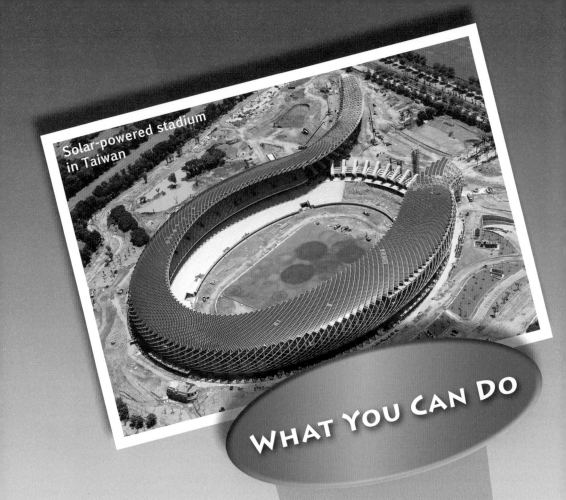

Solar-powered stadium in Taiwan

WHAT YOU CAN DO

Using solar energy sounds like a great way to power your home, but trying to convince your parents to put solar panels on the roof may not be so easy. Remember that solar panels are expensive. It may not be affordable for your family to buy and install them. But if your family is building a new home or making home renovations, you can suggest using solar panels. You can tell your family how solar energy is clean and does not pollute the environment—and how the family will no longer get an electric bill from the power company. In fact, if your home produces more electricity than your family uses, your parents can sell the extra electricity to the power company. Instead of a bill, they'll receive a check.

You might not be able to make your whole house run on solar power. One easy thing some people have done is

Chapter **5**

Solar parking meter

Cemetery near Barcelona, Spain

install solar lights outside their home, such as for walkways and spotlights. Another step is installing a solar-powered water heater.

According to the U.S. Department of Energy, a solar water heater is an efficient way to save money and reduce your family's carbon footprint. During a twenty-year period, one solar water heater can save more than 50 tons of carbon dioxide emissions. Manufacturers make solar water heaters for all types of climates. In areas of the world where it is warm and sunny most of the year, people can use passive solar water heaters, which warm the water with the heat of the sun and store it until it is needed.

Active solar water heaters have tubes to collect the warm water, and pumps that move the warm water to faucets or storage areas. In 2009, the average cost of installing a solar

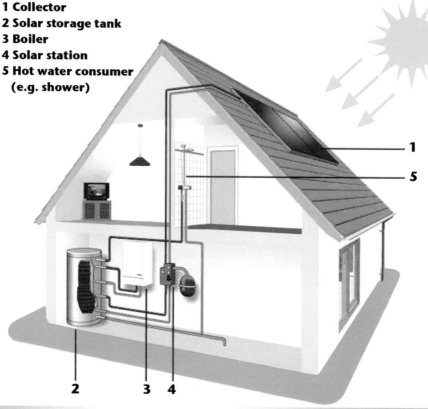

1 **Collector**
2 **Solar storage tank**
3 **Boiler**
4 **Solar station**
5 **Hot water consumer**
  (e.g. shower)

A household solar water heater uses solar panels to collect the sun's energy and warm the water. It does not generate electricity. It can save homeowners 50 to 85 percent of the hot-water portion of their utility bills.

water heater was $2,500. The average cost of installing a gas or electric water heater was about $900. But over time, the solar water heater would save a great deal of money in electric bills. Heating water is the third largest energy expense in your home. It is usually about 13 to 17 percent of your total utility bill. Over time, a solar water heater will save energy and money.

Even if your family cannot put up solar panels, or install a solar water heater, you can still use solar energy. Passive solar energy can be used by anyone. It does not need solar cells.

You can use the heat of the sun to warm your house by leaving window blinds open on sunny winter days. The sun will warm the rooms in your house, so you will not have to run your heater as much. When it is sunny and hot, you should keep the blinds closed. This will help keep the house cool, and your air conditioner will not have to work so hard.

Instead of using a clothes dryer, try using passive solar power. Dry your clothes by hanging them outside on a clothesline. The sun will do the drying, and your clothes will smell great.

You can also help make your house more energy efficient. Ed Begley Jr. advises people to start making easy energy changes. These changes can reduce the electricity your house uses. They will help the environment and save money. Parents love to save money.

Planting trees can help you use less energy. Trees can protect a house from the strong rays of the sun. They keep the house much cooler in the summer. One shade tree can reduce your summer cooling costs by 25 percent. Trees also act as a windbreak when it is cold and windy in the winter. The trees block the wind, and your house will stay warmer. Leafy shade trees should be planted on the south and west side of the house, and evergreens to block the wind should be planted on the north.

You can help save energy by growing a garden around your house. Bushes and plants around the foundation of the house are also helpful. They act as a windbreak and offer some shade.

Your family can save energy by adding insulation to the walls and attic. Insulation is a material that stops heat from entering or leaving a house. It keeps the house cool in the summer and warm in the winter. It is an earth-friendly way to save money and energy.

Ceiling fans are another way to reduce the amount of energy used in the house. Ceiling fans circulate the air and keep the house cool. It takes much less energy to run a ceiling fan than to run an air conditioner.

Installing a programmable thermostat is another way to save energy. A programmable thermostat automatically changes

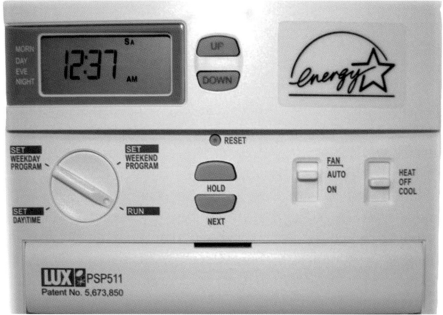

Programmable Thermostat Setpoints and Temperatures

Setting	Time	Setpoint Thermostat (Heat)	Setpoint Thermostat (Cool)
Wake	6:00 a.m.	≤ 70° F	≥ 78°F
Day	8:00 a.m.	Set back at least 8°F	Set up at least 7°F
Evening	6:00 p.m.	≤ 70° F	≥ 78°F
Sleep	10:00 p.m.	Set back at least 8°F	Set up at least 7°F

the temperature at which the furnace or air conditioner will turn on. You can set it to very specific times and temperatures. In cold weather, you can set it to switch to a lower temperature when everyone is at school or work. This will save energy and money by not running the heater as much when no one is home. In warm weather, you can set the thermostat to switch to a higher temperature, which will keep the air conditioner from running as much when no one is home. In both cases, you can program it to return the house to a comfortable temperature just before you get home. You can also have it adjust the temperature while you are sleeping. According to the Environmental Protection Agency (EPA), a programmable thermostat that is correctly programmed can reduce 1,847 pounds—nearly 1 ton—of greenhouse gas emissions per year per home.

Remember that you can also save energy and help the environment by turning off the lights when you don't need them, and turning off the television or computer when you are not using them. Better yet, unplug any electrical appliance that is not being used. Many appliances, especially computers, television sets, and CD players, draw power even when they're turned off. So do chargers for cell phones and electronic games. Unplug them unless you need to charge something.

Go through your house with your family and check to make sure appliances such as dishwashers and washing machines are in good repair. When it comes time to replace appliances, help your family choose energy-efficient ones. Appliances that earn the Energy Star label use less electricity and are kinder to the earth than most older models.

Changing the lightbulbs in your house can save energy. The Environmental Protection Agency urges people to replace their standard lightbulbs with new compact fluorescent lightbulbs. The fluorescent bulbs use 75 percent less energy

than standard bulbs, and they last 10 times as long. However, some environmental activists point out that the compact bulbs contain the chemical mercury. Mercury is a toxic substance that can cause nerve damage to people and animals. When the lightbulbs break, the mercury is released and can contaminate the ground or water.

The EPA admits that this is a concern but also points out that the use of compact fluorescent bulbs reduces the overall amount of mercury that goes into the environment. Traditional electric lightbulbs require a great deal more electricity, and coal-fired power plants are the biggest source of mercury emissions to the air. The EPA is working with states and manufacturers to find efficient ways to recycle compact fluorescent bulbs.

An easy way to save electricity is to paint your walls a light color. Light colors reflect light, so you don't need to turn on as many lamps.

Don't forget to recycle. It takes less energy to recycle an aluminum can than it does to make one from raw materials. Recycling also keeps the earth clean by reducing the waste taken to landfills. Recycled plastic and paper can be used to make things like carpet, furniture, and more paper. It all saves energy. And the less energy people use, the cleaner the planet.

Once you have taught your family about solar energy and ways to help the environment, you can teach people in your neighborhood. You can also help your school to become solar educated. Talk to your teachers and principal. Ask them if your class can study solar power. Research and write reports on solar energy. Present the reports to your class and school to tell them about the benefits of solar energy. You could even host a solar energy fair at your school.

SOLAR EXTRAS

Solar watch

Solar flashlight

Solar lawnmower

Solar yard light

Solar backpack

Portable solar panels

Invite people from the community to learn how solar power can save money and energy.

The more people who learn about solar power, the more they will want to use solar energy in their homes. People will realize that Ed Begley Jr. is right. Solar power is a great energy source. Using the power of the sun to produce electricity makes the world a cleaner place. It reduces pollution and slows the use of nonrenewable resources such as oil and gas.

In the future, the world may be full of solar homes. And your home just might be one of them.

Try This! Build a Solar Oven

Now you can cook like Ed Begley Jr. You can make your own solar oven with just a cardboard box and aluminum foil.

Solar oven

Materials
Cardboard box with a lid
   (a pizza box works well)
Plastic wrap
Glue and tape
Brushes for painting and gluing
Scissors
Ruler
String
Mat black paint
Shredded newspaper
Plastic film
Plastic zipper bag
Hot dog
Sunshine

Pizza box solar oven

1. Cut a three-sided flap in the top of your cardboard box.
2. Line the inside of the box with aluminum foil. Then place a layer of newspaper on top of the foil. Make sure the newspaper lies flat.
3. Cover the newspaper and the entire inside of the box with another layer of foil. Paint the foil black.
4. Fold back the flap along the uncut side and glue aluminum foil to the inside of the flap. Make sure the foil is shiny side out.
5. Measure a piece of plastic film to fit over the opening. The plastic must be larger than the hole. Tape the plastic to form a tight seal.
6. Place a hot dog in a plastic zipper bag. Put the bag inside the solar oven. Make sure the oven is in bright sun and that the flap is reflecting light into the box. If you need to, you can prop the lid of the box open with your ruler.
7. Let the sun cook your hot dog. It should be ready to eat in 15 minutes.

HISTORICAL TIMELINE

600 BCE A Greek named Thales of Miletus discovers static electricity.

1600 CE English scientist William Gilbert publishes a treatise on magnetism and invents the terms *electricity, electric force, magnetic pole,* and *electric attraction.*

1660 Otto von Guericke invents a machine that produces static electricity—the first electrical generator.

1752 Benjamin Franklin better understands electricity after flying a kite in a thunderstorm.

1786 Luigi Galvani discovers the electrical impulses of animal nerves while dissecting a frog.

1800 Alessandro Volta invents the voltaic pile—the first battery.

1831 Michael Faraday invents the dynamo to induce electricity.

1839 French scientist Edmond Becquerel discovers the photovoltaic effect.

1873 Willoughby Smith discovers the photoconductivity of selenium.

1879 Thomas Edison develops the electric lightbulb.

1891 Clarence Kemp patents the first commercial solar water heater.

1905 Albert Einstein publishes his paper on the photoelectric effect.

1915 Alfred Mellowes starts Guardian Frigerato to build first self-contained refrigerator for home use. His company is later renamed Frigidaire.

1920 The number of automobiles in the U.S. exceeds nine million.

1936 American inventor Charles Greeley Abbott invents an efficient solar boiler.

1939 The General Electric Company introduces first fluorescent lamp at the World's Fair in New York.

1944 American engineer Maria Telkes designs a portable solar-powered seawater distiller for military use.

1954 In Bell Labs, Daryl Chapin, Calvin Fuller, and Gerald Pearson work on the silicon voltaic cell, the first solar cell capable of changing enough sunlight into electricity to be able to run everyday electrical appliances.

1959 Silicon solar cells are used on the *Explorer VI* satellite.

1970 The first Earth Day is held on April 22.

1970s Elliot Berman designs a solar cell that greatly reduces the cost of solar energy.

1973 The University of Delaware builds Solar One, the first house to use solar panels to make electricity.

1981 The first solar-powered airplane flies over the English Channel.

1996 The University of Delaware builds Solar Two; this house has solar storage batteries.

2000 In November, astronauts begin living on the solar-powered International Space Station.

2001 NASA's sun-powered Helios Environmental Research aircraft sets a high-flying record of 96,863 feet (over 18 miles straight up).

2008 The solar-powered Quaranta concept car is unveiled.

2009 The world's first solar-hybrid power plant opens in Israel. Using both concentrated solar power and a hybrid microturbine, it generates power 24 hours a day.

FURTHER READING

For Young Readers

Armentrout, David, and Patricia. *Solar Energy*. Vero Beach, FL: Rourke Publishing, 2008.

Benduhn, Tea. *Solar Power (Energy for Today)*. New York: Gareth Stevens Publishing, 2008.

David, Laurie, and Cambria Gordon. *Down-to-Earth Guide to Global Warming*. New York: Orchard Books, 2007.

Graham, Ian. *Energy Forever? Solar Power*. Austin, TX: Steck-Vaughn, 2000.

Hirschmann, Kris. *Solar Energy (Our Environment)*. Chicago: Kidhaven Press, 2005.

Oxlade, Chris. *Solar Energy Fueling the Future*. Chicago: Heinemann Library, 2008.

Walker, Nicki. *Harnessing Power from the Sun*. New York: Crabtree Publishing, 2007.

WORKS CONSULTED

Archer, David. *Global Warming: Understanding the Forecast*. Malden, MA: Wiley-Blackwell, 2006.

Begley, Ed, Jr. *Living Like Ed*. New York: Clarkson Potter Publishers, 2008.

Bradford, Travis. *Solar Revolution: The Economic Transformation of the Global Energy Industry*. Cambridge, MA: MIT Press, 2006.

Chiras, Daniel D. *The Solar House*. White River Junction, VT: Chelsea Green Publishing, 2002.

DeGunther, Rik. *Solar Power Your Home for Dummies*. Hoboken, NJ: For Dummies Publishing, 2007.

Energy Information Administration. *Electric Power Monthly*. March 2009. http://www.eia.doe.gov/cneaf/electricity/epm/epm_sum.html

Ewing, Rex A., and Doug Pratt. *Got Sun? Go Solar*. Masonville, CO: PixyJack Press, 2005.

PHOTO CREDITS: p. 1—Beatrice Munch/cc-by-2.0; pp. 4, 6—AP Photo/Reed Saxon; p. 5 (Edward Norton)—Environmental Media Association, (solar house)—Gray Watson/cc-by-sa-3.0; pp. 7, 28—U.S. Department of Energy; p. 8 (chart)—Sharon Beck, (statistics)—Energy Information Administration, Annual Energy Review; pp. 10, 14—Sharon Beck; pp. 12, 32—Solar Cooking Archive; p. 13 (generators)—Lester Lefkowtiz/Corbis; p. 16—Stefan Kühn/GFDL/cc-by-sa-3.0; p. 20—Bob Rhine/NASA; p. 21 (photovoltaic effect)—RESLAB; p. 21 (Solar One)—University of Delaware; p. 22—GuidoB/cc-by-sa-3.0; pp. 23, 25—NASA; p. 29—Getty; p. 31—Koza1983/cc-by-3.0; p. 35 (parking meter)—Pilatus/GFDL/cc-by-sa-3.0. Every effort has been made to locate all copyright holders of material used in this book. If any errors or omissions have occurred, corrections will be made in future editions of the book.

Harper, Gavin D. J. *Solar Energy Projects for Evil Genius*. New York: McGraw-Hill, 2007.

Murphy, Meghan. "Solar Celebrity and Affordable Housing." *Renewable Energy World*, July 23, 2007. http://www.renewableenergyworld. com/rea/news/story?id=49387

The Prince's Foundation Policy and Research http://www.princes-foundation.org/

Ramsey, Dan. *The Complete Idiot's Guide to Solar Power for Your Home*. New York: Penguin Group, 2007.

ON THE INTERNET

Green-planet-solar-energy.com: *Solar Power Facts* http://www.green-planet-solar-energy.com/

NASA: "Sun-powered Wing Brushes Against Space!" http://spaceplace.nasa.gov/en/kids/helios_fact.shtml

Plans for Solar Cookers http://www.solarcooking.org/plans/

Ranger Rick's Green Zone http://www.nwf.org/rrgreenzone/Default.aspx

Solar 4 Schools: *Solar Power at Home* http://www.solar4schools.co.uk/kids/Solar-Power-At-Home

Solar Energy International: *Kid's Information* http://www.solarenergy.org/resources/youngkids.html

U.S. Department of Energy, Kid's Home Page: "About Renewable Energy" http://www.eere.energy.gov/kids/renergy.html

U.S. Department of Energy: *Roofus' Solar and Efficient Home* http://www1.eere.energy.gov/kids/roofus/

Solar Tent, concept

GLOSSARY

active solar energy (AK-tiv SOH-lar EN-er-jee)—Solar radiation used to provide space heating, hot water, or electricity.

atom (AT-om)—One of the basic building blocks for all matter.

carbon footprint—The amount of pollution caused by a person, home, or business.

electromagnetic induction (ee-LEK-troh-mag-NEH-tik in-DUK-shun)—Using magnets to cause electricity to flow through coiled wires.

electron (ee-LEK-tron)—A basic part of an atom that contains a negative charge of electricity.

extinct (ek-STINKT)—No longer exisitng.

fossil fuel (FAH-sil fyool)—Any carbon-containing fuel that comes from the decomposed remains of plants and animals, including oil, petroleum, coal, and natural gas.

global warming (GLOH-bul WAR-ming)—An increase in the world's temperatures caused by the greenhouse effect.

greenhouse effect—The trapping of heat on Earth's surface by extra atmospheric gases, such as carbon dioxide and methane.

nonrenewable energy (non-ree-noo-uh-bul EH-ner-jee)—Energy sources that have a limited supply.

passive solar (PAA-siv SOH-lar)—Using the sun directly for heat.

photovoltaic (foh-toh-vol-TAY-ik) **energy**—Sunlight used to produce electricity. It is often abbreviated PV.

primary energy source (PRY-mayr-ee EH-ner-jee sors)—Substances that occur in nature and can be used to produce energy, such as coal, oil, and wind.

radiation (ray-dee-AY-shun)—The flow of energy across open space.

radioactive (ray-dee-oh-AK-tiv)—Having a huge amount of stored but unstable energy.

renewable energy (ree-NOO-uh-bul EH-ner-jee)—Energy obtained from a source that can be used again and again.

silicon (SIH-lih-kon)—A natural element found in sand.

solar array (SOH-lar uh-RAY)—A large number of solar panels used to gather and store energy from the sun.

solar energy—Energy obtained from the light and heat of the sun.

solar thermal energy—Heat energy from the sun.

turbine (TUR-bun *or* TUR-byn)—A machine with blades that are moved by wind, steam, or water. When the blades turn, they produce electrical or mechanical power.

INDEX

Stephanie Bearce grew up on the wide-open plains of the Midwest. There was plenty of sunshine and wind. Her neighbors built a passive solar home right in the hill of a pasture. That house was fascinating. When she grew up and went to college, she studied science. Solar homes were just starting to become popular, and she took an ecology class that taught about solar energy. As an adult she worked as a teacher. She taught children about the amazing resource. Now Bearce lives in Missouri, and she is still fascinated by solar homes. She says, "I don't have one right now, but maybe someday I will."